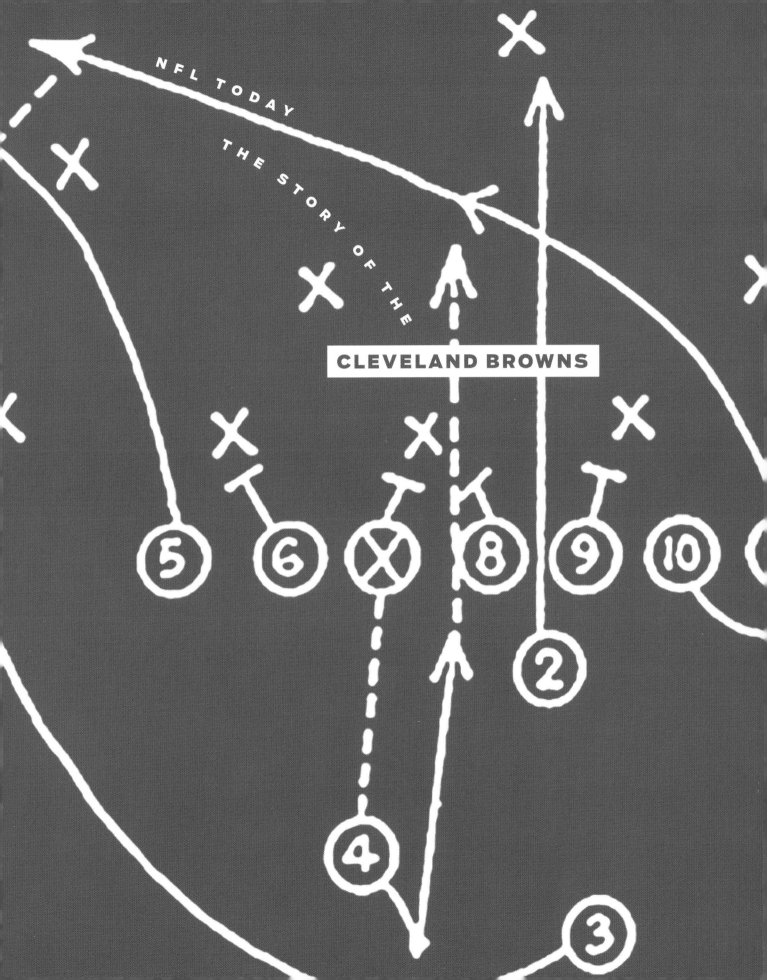

NFL TODAY

THE STORY OF THE

CLEVELAND BROWNS

THE STORY OF THE CLEVELAND BROWNS

SARA GILBERT

CREATIVE EDUCATION

PUBLISHED BY CREATIVE EDUCATION
P.O. BOX 227, MANKATO, MINNESOTA 56002
CREATIVE EDUCATION IS AN IMPRINT OF THE CREATIVE COMPANY
WWW.THECREATIVECOMPANY.US

DESIGN AND PRODUCTION BY BLUE DESIGN
ART DIRECTION BY RITA MARSHALL
PRINTED IN THE UNITED STATES OF AMERICA

PHOTOGRAPHS BY CORBIS (MARK DUNCAN/AP),
GETTY IMAGES (BRIAN BAHR, KIMBERLY BARTH/
AFP, AL BELLO, JONATHAN DANIEL, DAVID DERMER/
DIAMOND IMAGES, STEPHEN DUNN, FOCUS ON
SPORT, GEORGE GOJKOVICH, BOB GOMEL/TIME &
LIFE PICTURES, DAVID MAXWELL/AFP, JIM MCISAAC,
RONALD C. MODRA/SPORTS IMAGERY, NFL, HY
PESKIN/SPORTS ILLUSTRATED, PRO FOOTBALL HALL
OF FAME/NFL, JOE ROBBINS, J. BAYLOR ROBERTS/
NATIONAL GEOGRAPHIC, GEORGE ROSE, GREGORY
SHAMUS, PAUL SPINELLI, MATT SULLIVAN, TONY
TOMSIC/NFL, JIM TURNER/NFL, RON VESELY, JOHN
ZICH/AFP)

COPYRIGHT © 2014 CREATIVE EDUCATION

LIBRARY OF CONGRESS CATALOGING-IN-PUBLICATION DATA
GILBERT, SARA.
THE STORY OF THE CLEVELAND BROWNS / SARA GILBERT.
P. CM. — (NFL TODAY)
INCLUDES INDEX.
SUMMARY: THE HISTORY OF THE NATIONAL FOOTBALL LEAGUE'S
CLEVELAND BROWNS, SURVEYING THE FRANCHISE'S BIGGEST
STARS AND MOST MEMORABLE MOMENTS FROM ITS INAUGURAL
SEASON IN 1946 TO TODAY.
ISBN 978-1-60818-299-2
1. CLEVELAND BROWNS (FOOTBALL TEAM: 1946-1995)—HISTORY—
JUVENILE LITERATURE. I. TITLE.

GV956.C6G56 2013
796.332'640977132—DC23   2012028443

FIRST EDITION
9 8 7 6 5 4 3 2 1

COVER: RUNNING BACK TRENT RICHARDSON
PAGE 2: QUARTERBACK BRANDON WEEDEN
PAGES 4–5: WIDE RECEIVER JOSH CRIBBS
PAGE 6: FULLBACK JIM BROWN

TABLE OF CONTENTS

SIDELINE STORIES

MEET THE BROWNS

CLEVELAND HAS EARNED FAME FOR ITS STEEL AND IRON PRODUCTION

Big Browns

Cleveland, Ohio, had a big beginning. Because it was built at the southern edge of Lake Erie, it became a busy Great Lakes shipping hub almost immediately. The completion of the Erie Canal in 1825 and the expansion of America's railroads further established its prominence as a port city, leading to rapid population growth that peaked at almost one million in the mid-1900s. Unfortunately, that boom ended when a long period of social unrest, economic hardship, and industrial change hit Cleveland. In recent years, however, the city has rebounded. Now it has emerged as a growing cultural hub and is again considered one of the most livable cities in America.

Like their hometown, the Cleveland Browns professional football team also had a big beginning in 1946. Led by Paul Brown, a much-revered college coach who was the inspiration for the team's name, the Browns became the most dominant team in the All-America Football Conference (AAFC). Brown had handpicked a roster that featured several of his former college players as well as those whom he had both feared and admired as

OTTO GRAHAM BECAME A CLEVELAND ICON AS AN EARLY BROWNS SUPERSTAR

Paul Brown

COACH / BROWNS SEASONS: 1946–62

Paul Brown could have become a lawyer. Instead, he became a football coach—one of the greatest of all time. His first coaching job was at a naval academy prep school in Maryland, where he compiled a record of 16–1–1 in two years. That success was enough to make Brown scrap his plans for law school and put his energies into coaching instead. Before long, the Ohio native had moved up to the college ranks and, in 1945, was asked to lead the brand-new Cleveland Browns team. But Brown was hardly a traditional coach. In addition to using intelligence tests to screen potential players, he also built a library of game film and studied it regularly. A former teacher, he herded his players into classrooms for instruction and used a radio transmitter to communicate with players on the field. Brown's tactics broke new ground at the time and helped him assemble a 167–53–8 record during his 17 seasons with the Browns. "He's certainly one of the key figures in professional sports," said Cincinnati Bengals quarterback Ken Anderson. "Football would not be what it is without him."

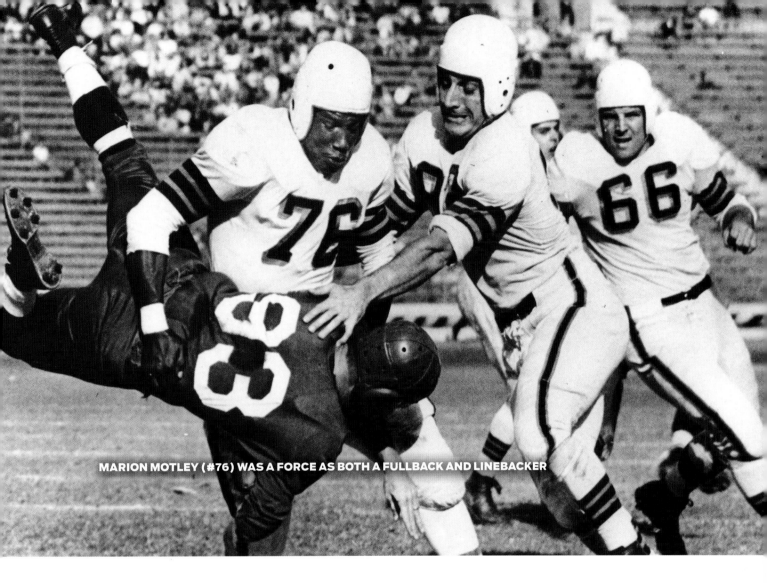

MARION MOTLEY (#76) WAS A FORCE AS BOTH A FULLBACK AND LINEBACKER

opponents—including his star player, quarterback Otto Graham from Chicago's Northwestern University.

With Graham under center, hulking fullback Marion Motley carrying the ball, and lanky receiver Mac Speedie hauling in seven touchdowns in 1946, Cleveland compiled a 12–2 record and won the first AAFC championship. In 1947, the Browns again won 12 games; in 1948, they won all 14 contests that they played. By the end of the 1949 season, the Browns had put together a combined 52–4–3 record and had won all four AAFC championships. But when the AAFC ceased operations before the start of the 1950 season, few people believed the Browns could continue their domination in the National Football League (NFL).

Paul Brown wasn't worried, though, and his confidence inspired his players as well. The Browns' convincing 35–10 win over the defending NFL champion Philadelphia Eagles in the first game of the 1950 season also inspired the fans. The underdog Browns scored a touchdown on their first offensive possession, and Graham threw for 346 yards and 3 touchdowns. "We were so fired up," Graham remembered. "We would have played them for a keg of beer or a chocolate milk shake."

With the help of powerful defensive end Len Ford and center Frank Gatski, the Browns put together a 10–2 season in 1950 that culminated in a 30–28 victory over the Los Angeles Rams in the NFL Championship Game. Cleveland went on to win the NFL Eastern Conference title for five more years, capturing league championships in 1954 and 1955. The NFL Championship Game against the Rams in 1955 was Graham's last; after throwing two touchdowns and running for two more, he left the game to a standing ovation at Los Angeles Memorial Coliseum.

Graham's departure was followed by Cleveland's first losing season, a 5–7 campaign in 1956. But it also opened the door for a new superstar to emerge: running back Jim Brown, a 6-foot-2 and 232-pound powerhouse drafted by the Browns in 1957. With a frightening combination of speed and strength, he ran for 942 yards and scored 10 touchdowns as a rookie. The following year, he nearly doubled those numbers. Before the end of his NFL career, Brown would gain 12,312 total rushing yards, score 126 touchdowns, and win an incredible 8 league rushing titles.

Brown's running heroics took some of the pressure off the string of quarterbacks, including Milt Plum, who tried to replace Graham. The team rode Brown's shoulders to a division title in 1957 and made it to the playoffs again in 1958. In 1959, Brown led the NFL with 1,329 rushing yards, and in 1960, Plum threw 21 touchdowns, but the team missed the playoffs both times.

The late 1950s and early '60s were disappointing years for Cleveland fans accustomed to winning championships. Owner David Jones was unhappy, too. In 1961, he sold the Browns to former television producer Art Modell, who quickly clashed with Coach Brown. Brown's no-nonsense style had also rubbed some younger players, including Jim Brown, the wrong way. When the 1962 season ended with a mediocre 7–6–1 record, Modell fired Cleveland's longtime coach and hired Blanton Collier to take his place.

Collier's looser style—evident in his decision to allow quarterback Frank Ryan to call the plays himself—led to back-to-back 10-win seasons in 1963 and 1964. The Browns met the heavily favored Baltimore Colts in the 1964 NFL Championship Game and successfully stifled the Colts' star quarterback, Johnny Unitas. Ryan, meanwhile, threw three touchdown passes to his reliable wingman Gary Collins,

Naming the Browns

The first order of business after Arthur "Mickey" McBride purchased a professional football franchise for Cleveland was to find it a coach—and McBride quickly fixed on local hero Paul Brown, who had led Ohio State University to a national college championship in 1942. The next item on the agenda was to select a name for the team—but as it turned out, that went right along with finding its coach. McBride offered a $1,000 war bond to the person who could select the best name for the team. Many of the entries suggested that the team be called the Browns, in honor of its beloved coach. But that made Paul Brown uncomfortable, and McBride instead paid the $1,000 to a fan who had recommended "Cleveland Panthers." Unfortunately, that didn't work, either; an NFL team had used that name in 1926 and still owned the rights. McBride went back to the fans' first choice: the Cleveland Browns. Although Paul Brown maintained that the name was in honor of boxer Joe "The Brown Bomber" Louis, he later acknowledged that it was for himself instead.

CLEVELAND TOOK ITS TEAM NAME FROM THE DAPPER PAUL BROWN (RIGHT)

ERNIE GREEN (RIGHT) HELPED JIM BROWN CARRY CLEVELAND'S RUSHING LOAD

and Lou Groza added two field goals to win the game 27–0.

I n 1965, Brown rushed for more than 1,500 yards and won NFL Most Valuable Player (MVP) honors as he led the team back to the NFL Championship Game. But after the Browns lost to the Green Bay Packers, the 30-year-old running back announced his retirement. Brown left the game as the NFL's all-time leading rusher; nearly two decades would pass before legendary Chicago Bears running back Walter Payton topped Brown's total yardage. "It is possible that had Brown continued to play, he would have put all the league's rushing records so far out of reach that they would have been only a distant dream … to the runners who followed him," *Sports Illustrated* reporter Peter King later noted.

Otto Graham

QUARTERBACK / BROWNS SEASONS: 1946–55 / HEIGHT: 6-FOOT-1 / WEIGHT: 196 POUNDS

Illinois native Otto Graham went to Chicago's Northwestern University on a basketball scholarship. One day, the football coach saw him throwing a football for fun and talked him into joining the team. That decision launched a Hall of Fame career that would span 10 years and include 3 NFL and 4 AAFC championships. Graham was one of the premier quarterbacks of his era, throwing 174 career touchdowns and being elected to the Pro Bowl 5 times. Graham's dominance on the gridiron was so complete that when he announced his retirement after the 1954 season, coach Paul Brown personally begged him to return. In Graham's encore season, he led the Browns to a 9–2–1 record and a 38–14 victory over the Los Angeles Rams in the NFL Championship Game on December 26, 1955. Upon his death in 2003, Graham was described as "an absolute model of character and integrity" by Pro Football Hall of Fame president John Bankert. He is widely considered one of the greatest football players of all time, and his number 14 jersey is one of only five that have been retired by the Browns.

The Unbeatable Browns

The Cleveland Browns clearly dominated the AAFC. During the conference's four years of existence, the Browns lost only four games. But there was one season during that period in which the Browns didn't lose or tie a game at all—1948. After winning the first game of the season by a 5-point margin, the team won the next 8 by an average of 18 points each. Although subsequent games against the San Francisco 49ers and Brooklyn Dodgers were not quite as lopsided, the Browns continued to win. However remarkable the streak, fans remained unimpressed. As the contests became less competitive and less evenly matched, crowds for the games both at home and away began to dwindle. Fewer than 10,000 fans showed up for the season finale against the Brooklyn Dodgers, and only 22,000 attended the AAFC Championship Game between the Browns and the Buffalo Bills two weeks later. The unbeatable Browns may have been the AAFC's downfall; in the wake of declining attendance numbers, the league merged with the NFL in 1950.

THE BROWNS OF THE AAFC WENT DOWN AS ONE OF THE GREATEST DYNASTIES IN SPORTS

New Beginning, Sad Endings

Running back Leroy Kelly made a valiant effort to compensate for Brown's absence. Thanks to his fast feet and receiver Paul Warfield's sure hands, the Browns made it back to the NFL Championship Game in 1968 and 1969. The sting of losing those games was compounded when Cleveland also lost Coach Collier, whose failing health caused him to retire at the end of the 1970 season.

Although Cleveland made it to the playoffs in 1971 and 1972, the personnel losses began to take a toll. As young quarterback Mike Phipps struggled to learn the ropes, the Browns recorded consecutive losing seasons in 1974 and 1975. Hope returned when coach Forrest Gregg promoted backup quarterback Brian Sipe to the starting position in 1976. The Browns went 6–8 in 1977, then 8–8 in 1978. By 1979, Sipe and the Browns had earned a reputation as a team capable of

BRIAN SIPE PEAKED IN 1980, CAPTURING THE NFL MVP AWARD THAT SEASON

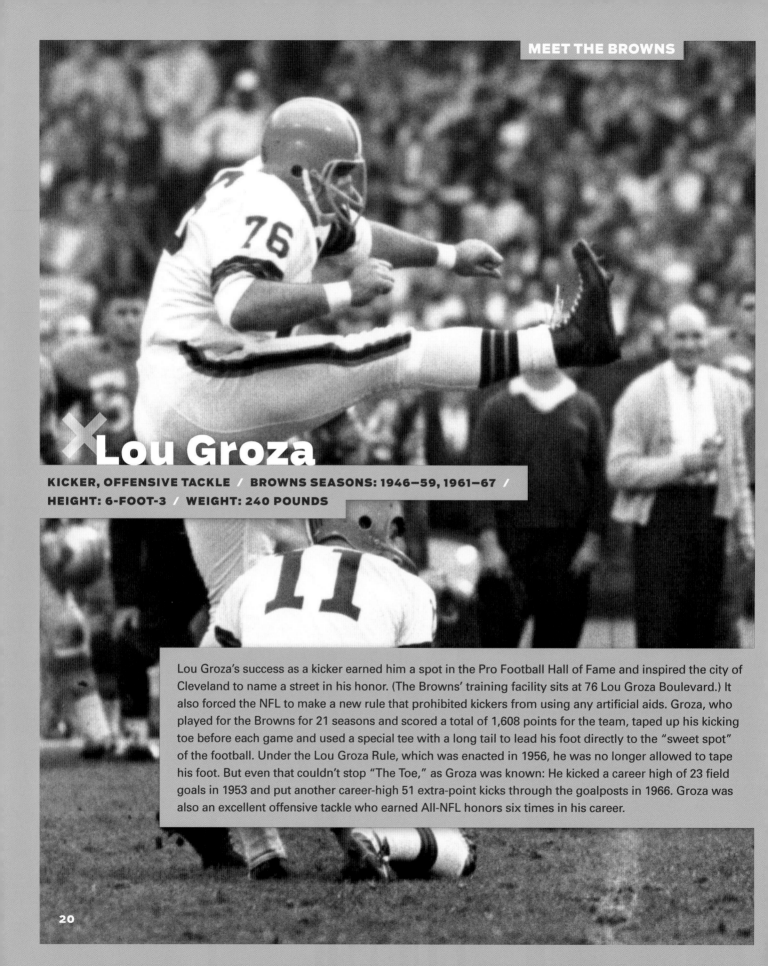

Lou Groza

**KICKER, OFFENSIVE TACKLE / BROWNS SEASONS: 1946–59, 1961–67 /
HEIGHT: 6-FOOT-3 / WEIGHT: 240 POUNDS**

Lou Groza's success as a kicker earned him a spot in the Pro Football Hall of Fame and inspired the city of Cleveland to name a street in his honor. (The Browns' training facility sits at 76 Lou Groza Boulevard.) It also forced the NFL to make a new rule that prohibited kickers from using any artificial aids. Groza, who played for the Browns for 21 seasons and scored a total of 1,608 points for the team, taped up his kicking toe before each game and used a special tee with a long tail to lead his foot directly to the "sweet spot" of the football. Under the Lou Groza Rule, which was enacted in 1956, he was no longer allowed to tape his foot. But even that couldn't stop "The Toe," as Groza was known: He kicked a career high of 23 field goals in 1953 and put another career-high 51 extra-point kicks through the goalposts in 1966. Groza was also an excellent offensive tackle who earned All-NFL honors six times in his career.

coming from behind to win with last-minute heroics. After achieving dramatic, heart-stopping finishes to several games during that 9–7 season, fans began referring to the club as the "Kardiac Kids."

The Browns, led by coach Sam Rutigliano, entered the 1980 season loaded with talent, from sure-handed tight end Ozzie Newsome to punishing defensive end Lyle Alzado. But Sipe was the undisputed star. Fans were so confident in their young quarterback that they began predicting a trip to the "Siper Bowl." Sipe didn't disappoint—he threw for more than 4,000 yards and 30 touchdowns and earned the NFL MVP award as the Browns won the American Football Conference (AFC) Central Division with an 11–5 record.

That record secured home-field advantage for the Browns in the playoffs, which meant that any AFC team hoping to reach the Super Bowl would have to battle both the bitter weather at Cleveland Municipal Stadium and the unrelenting Browns. The Oakland Raiders managed to emerge victorious in the first round of the playoffs. Sipe tossed an errant pass that landed in the hands of an Oakland player and ended a Cleveland comeback late in the game. Although the team's Super Bowl dreams ended with that interception, Sipe stayed positive. "Yes, I have feelings of regret and despair about losing this game, but fused with them is the knowledge that we had a good year," he said. "I think we lifted the feelings of everybody around here."

Sipe's 1981 season left everyone feeling down, though. His 17 touchdowns were overshadowed by his 25 interceptions as the Browns finished at a disappointing 5–11. Sipe left Cleveland in 1983; a year later, Rutigliano was fired as head coach. Defensive coordinator Marty Schottenheimer took up the coaching reins, and in 1985, he hung the hopes of the franchise on young quarterback and hometown hero Bernie Kosar, who had enjoyed a record-setting college career at the University of Miami before joining the Browns.

When starting quarterback Gary Danielson went down with an injury midway through the 1985 season, Kosar took over. Although he fumbled his first professional snap, Kosar won four of the six games he started. When the 1986 season began, he looked like a bona fide starter, slinging passes to such veteran receivers as Newsome and Brian Brennan and to the newest weapon waiting downfield:

Barking Like a Dawg

In 1985, defensive back Hanford Dixon ran around training camp barking like a dog. His bizarre behavior caught on with the crowds who had gathered to watch the Browns get ready for the season. Soon, fans in the bleacher section of Cleveland Municipal Stadium began wearing dog masks to the games and barking for their favorite team. Tickets to "The Dawg Pound," as that section has since been known, became some of the most coveted in the stadium, and the fans who sat there became known as some of the rowdiest spectators in all of sports. Some fans believe that they were even able to influence the outcome of a game against the Denver Broncos in 1989. After fans in The Dawg Pound started throwing bones and dog biscuits at Broncos players in the fourth quarter of a close game, the referees decided to have the teams switch sides of the field. That move allowed the Browns to play with the wind at their backs, which may have helped them drive down the field late in the game and kick a game-winning field goal.

COSTUMES AND FACE PAINT ARE PART OF THE FESTIVITIES IN THE DAWG POUND

GERALD McNEIL WAS PART OF AN IMPRESSIVE FLEET OF '80s BROWNS RECEIVERS

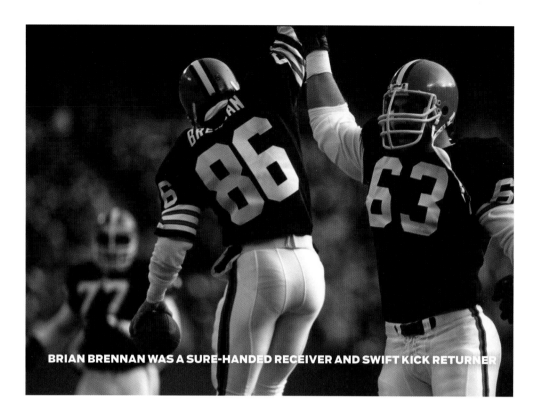

BRIAN BRENNAN WAS A SURE-HANDED RECEIVER AND SWIFT KICK RETURNER

wide receiver Webster Slaughter, who had been the Browns' top pick in the 1986 NFL Draft.

When the rebuilt Browns rolled to a 12–4 record and home-field advantage in the 1986 playoffs, Cleveland fans were confident that this would finally be their year, even after the Browns fell behind the New York Jets in the first round of the playoffs. On one play, Kosar was pounded to the ground by Jets defensive lineman Mark Gastineau and stood up more determined than ever. "I saw a look in his eyes I'd never seen before," Newsome recalled. "He was not going to be denied. He was going to find a way to win that football game."

Kosar and the Browns did find a way, scoring twice to force sudden-death overtime. Mark Moseley kicked a 27-yard field goal to make the final score 23–20, the team's first playoff win in 17 seasons. But Cleveland's luck ran out the following week, when it faced the Denver Broncos in the AFC Championship Game. Although the Browns held a 20–13 lead late into the fourth quarter, Broncos quarterback John Elway was able to tie the game with just seconds left on the clock. Then Elway led his team to a 23–20 overtime victory that left the 80,000 fans in Municipal Stadium devastated.

Elway and the Broncos returned to Cleveland for the AFC title game in 1987 as well. This time, the Browns fell behind early on, trailing by three touchdowns in the third quarter. Kosar led three scoring drives to tie the game 31–31 and had his team on the move deep in Denver territory when running back Earnest Byner fumbled the ball near the goal line. "It's tough to come back and tie the game and then lose," Kosar said afterwards. "It's not fun losing this game, much less two years in a row."

Draft Dodging

Bernie Kosar was expected to be one of the top picks in the NFL Draft in 1985, which meant that he would likely be selected by either the Buffalo Bills or the Minnesota Vikings. But Kosar, who grew up in Boardman, Ohio, had made it clear that he wanted to start his professional football career with his hometown team, the Cleveland Browns. The Browns, meanwhile, wanted to add Kosar and his strong throwing arm to their roster almost as much—but they knew he wouldn't be available when their turn to pick came up. So Kosar, who had just finished his junior year at the University of Miami, waited until after the deadline to declare his intention to enter the draft. That intentional delay made him eligible to participate in a supplemental draft, where the Browns had already been guaranteed to have the first shot at selecting him. Despite protests from other teams that wanted the talented young quarterback on their roster, Kosar was officially selected by the Browns on July 3, 1985, and immediately signed a five-year contract with the team.

BERNIE KOSAR GAVE CLEVELAND STEADY LEADERSHIP FOR NINE NFL SEASONS

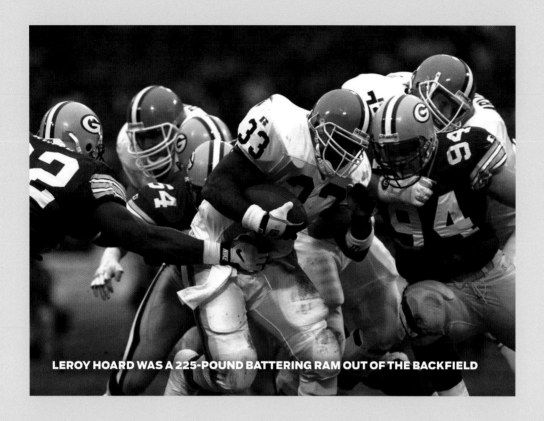

LEROY HOARD WAS A 225-POUND BATTERING RAM OUT OF THE BACKFIELD

The Browns Return

Cleveland remained one of the most powerful teams in the NFL for the rest of the 1980s—but Denver always seemed to be stronger. The bitter rivalry between the Browns and the Broncos was reinforced in 1989, when the two teams again met in the conference title game. This time, the Broncos led from start to finish, sealing their trip to the Super Bowl with a final touchdown in the fourth quarter and winning 37–21.

That would be the Browns' last chance for a championship. Kosar's skills started to slip, and the 1990s featured four consecutive losing seasons, starting with a 3–13 record in 1990. In 1990, Kosar threw only 10 touchdowns and 15 interceptions. Despite the emergence of running back Leroy Hoard, the team—including Kosar—continued to disappoint. After sitting out much of the 1992 season, Kosar was released in 1993.

Kosar's departure upset many Browns fans. That anger increased as rumors circulated that team owner Art Modell—who was unhappy with the team's accommodations in the

ERIC METCALF ELECTRIFIED BROWNS FANS WITH HIS PUNT RETURNS IN THE EARLY '90s

Jim Brown

RUNNING BACK / BROWNS SEASONS: 1957–65 / HEIGHT: 6-FOOT-2 / WEIGHT: 232 POUNDS

Jim Brown's budding acting career was the only thing that could have halted the hulking running back's successful football career. In 1965, Brown was 29 years old and just 9 years into his professional football career, but he already held several NFL records. He set the single-season rushing record with 1,863 yards in 1963 and held the career record (12,312) until Chicago Bears legend Walter Payton passed him in 1984. Although many of the records he set have since tumbled, Brown remains the only rusher in NFL history to have averaged more than 100 yards per game over his career. Unfortunately for football, Brown retired after team owner Art Modell ordered him to leave the movie set of *The Dirty Dozen* to report to training camp. The multitalented Brown, who was reportedly offered 42 athletic scholarships in everything from football to lacrosse when he graduated from high school, went on to appear in several movies and later provided color commentary for mixed martial arts fights. He was inducted into the Pro Football Hall of Fame in 1971.

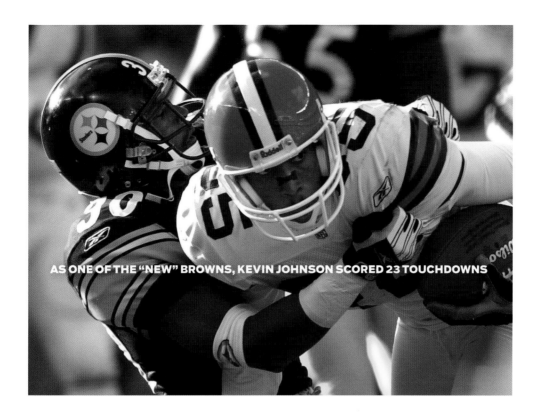
AS ONE OF THE "NEW" BROWNS, KEVIN JOHNSON SCORED 23 TOUCHDOWNS

aging Municipal Stadium—was considering relocating the team. On November 6, 1995, Modell made his intentions official when he announced that he was moving the franchise to Baltimore, Maryland.

Fan reaction was swift: more than 100 lawsuits were immediately filed, both by fans and by the city of Cleveland, which wanted to keep the proud Browns name, colors, and team history. Extensive negotiations between the NFL and city officials yielded an agreement that allowed Cleveland to retain the Browns' legacy, while Modell could keep the players under contract. The league promised to bring a new team to Cleveland by 1999 and to help fund a stadium for a new Browns squad to play in. Almost as soon as Modell left town, Cleveland started preparing for its beloved Browns to return.

In November 1996, Municipal Stadium was demolished to make way for the state-of-the-art Cleveland Browns Stadium. By early 1999, new owners Al Lerner and Carmen Policy had hired former Jacksonville Jaguars offensive coordinator Chris Palmer to coach the revived Browns team. The final pieces of the puzzle, the new players, began to be put in place once the Browns had selected quarterback Tim Couch with the first pick of the 1999 NFL Draft.

More than 73,000 fans crammed into Cleveland Browns Stadium to see Couch and his teammates, including wide receiver Kevin Johnson and safety Marquez Pope, start the 1999 season. Although hopes were not high for the new team, many of those fans couldn't hide their disappointment when the Browns were crushed 43–0 by the rival Pittsburgh Steelers. The offense managed to gain only 40 total yards, and Couch, who was sent into the game in the fourth quarter, started his professional career by throwing an interception.

More than a month would go by before the Browns recorded a victory, a 21–16 triumph over the Saints in New Orleans. But Couch's late-game heroics that October afternoon renewed the team's hopes for the future. The Browns were behind by 2 points with 21 seconds to go when Couch launched a 56-yard "Hail Mary" pass that landed in Johnson's arms. "It's a memory I'll never forget," Couch said. "I can remember [New Orleans coach] Mike Ditka lying on the carpet and seeing him as I was running down the sideline. That was probably the best part of all."

But Couch and Cleveland enjoyed the thrill of victory only once more during that disappointing first season, and things didn't improve much during the

PASSER TIM COUCH WAS THE CENTERPIECE OF THE BROWNS' REBUILDING EFFORTS

Broncos or Bust

Only the Denver Broncos stood between the Cleveland Browns and the Super Bowl in the late 1980s. In 1986 and 1987, the Browns squared off against the Broncos in the AFC Championship Game. Both times, improbable plays made the difference between winning and losing. In 1986, it was "The Drive," a methodical, 98-yard march down the field that was led by confident Broncos quarterback John Elway. Elway took five minutes to get near the end zone before passing to rookie Mark Jackson for a game-tying touchdown. Then Rich Karlis kicked a field goal for the win in overtime. In 1987, it was "The Fumble": With Denver up by seven points and one minute left on the clock, reliable Browns running back Earnest Byner took a handoff from quarterback Bernie Kosar just seven yards shy of the goal line. Byner was within a yard of the end zone when Broncos cornerback Jeremiah Castille stripped the ball from him and recovered the ensuing fumble. Four plays later, Denver surrendered an intentional safety to preserve a 38–33 lead, and the Browns went home disappointed once again.

THE BROWNS-BRONCOS PLAYOFF CLASHES IN THE '80s BROKE HEARTS IN CLEVELAND

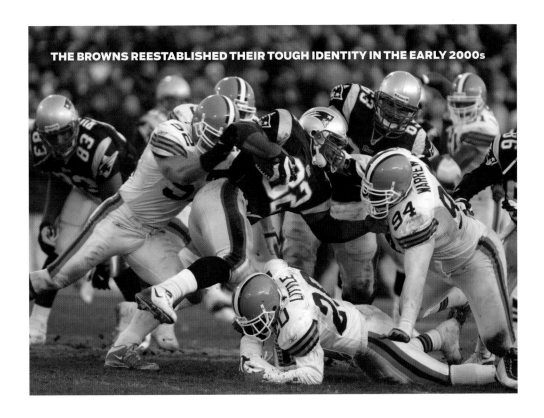

THE BROWNS REESTABLISHED THEIR TOUGH IDENTITY IN THE EARLY 2000s

2000 campaign. Couch threw seven touchdowns in seven games before being sidelined for the last nine games of the season with a broken thumb. The Browns won just one game without him and were shut out twice in the waning weeks of the season—including a 48–0 drubbing at the hands of the Jaguars. "I feel like I'm driving a runaway train," Coach Palmer remarked as the team went on a 0–5 skid to end with a 3–13 record.

By the end of the year, Palmer's train had run out of steam. He was fired, his two-year coaching tenure the shortest ever for an NFL expansion team. With new coach Butch Davis on the sidelines and hulking defensive end Courtney Brown on the field, the Browns improved to 7–9 in 2001. The following year, Couch and Brown hit their stride, and veterans such as tough safety Robert Griffith and offensive lineman Ross Verba gave the team balance. With a 9–7 record, the Browns earned their first playoff appearance since 1994. Although they were up 33–21 late in the fourth quarter in a game against Pittsburgh, the Steelers scored 15 unanswered points in the last 5 minutes to win 36–33.

Injuries and salary issues depleted the Browns' roster for the next two years, sending the team into a free fall that included a 5–11 record in 2003 and a 4–12 mark in 2004. Couch began struggling, and, after being forced to split time with backup Kelly Holcomb in 2003, he was released before the 2004 season. His replacement, Jeff Garcia, lasted only one season. With Johnson and most of the other Browns players obtained in 1999 also gone, the five-year-old team found itself in rebuilding mode already.

CLEVELAND DEFENSIVE LINEMEN GERARD WARREN (LEFT) AND COURTNEY BROWN

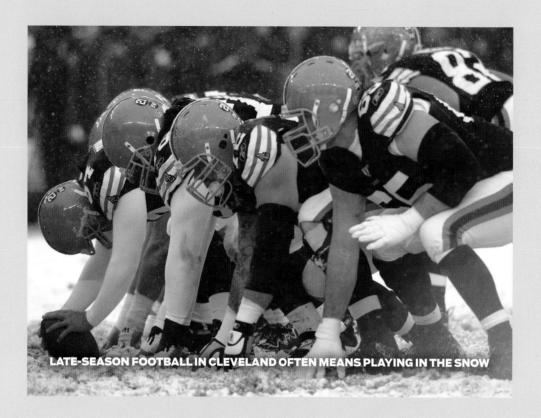

LATE-SEASON FOOTBALL IN CLEVELAND OFTEN MEANS PLAYING IN THE SNOW

Looking for Leaders

Befor the 2005 season, the Browns put the team in the hands of Romeo Crennel, who was named the 14th head coach in franchise history. Crennel had been the defensive coordinator for the New England Patriots when the Patriots won the Super Bowl in 2001, 2003, and 2004, and the Browns were hopeful that his experience would help improve Cleveland's fortunes. "The Browns are getting a good football coach and an even better man," Patriots linebacker Mike Vrabel said.

But Crennel had a lot of work to do in Cleveland. He inherited an ineffective offense that was able to score only 19 total touchdowns during the 2005 season. Although his Browns squad improved to 6–10 that year, Crennel knew that he needed to add talent to the roster before the start of the 2006 season. The Browns signed several free agents, including three Ohio natives—wide receiver Joe Jurevicius, center LeCharles Bentley, and offensive tackle Kevin Shaffer—who were all eager for the opportunity to play in Cleveland. But injuries at key positions crippled the team before the season started

JOE JUREVICIUS GAVE THE BROWNS VETERAN TOUGHNESS IN 2006 AND 2007

Ozzie Newsome

TIGHT END / BROWNS SEASONS: 1978–90 / HEIGHT: 6-FOOT-2 / WEIGHT: 232 POUNDS

In 1978, Ozzie "The Wizard of Oz" Newsome caught 38 passes for 589 yards—not bad for a rookie. In fact, those numbers were good enough to earn the young tight end the Browns' Offensive Player of the Year award, the first time in 25 years that a rookie had received the honor. But things only got better for Newsome. In 1979, he was named an All-Pro, and in 1981, when he made 69 catches for 1,002 yards and 6 touchdowns, he earned the first of 3 invitations to the Pro Bowl. Newsome played in 198 consecutive games for the Browns and caught at least 1 pass in 150 straight games, the second-longest streak in the NFL at the time of his retirement in 1990. But it may be what Newsome did after he left the field that will be his most lasting legacy: On November 22, 2002, he became the first African American general manager in the NFL when he assumed that position with the Baltimore Ravens. He was soon widely considered to be one of the best personnel evaluators in the game.

and continued to be a factor throughout the year. Instead of improving in 2006, the Browns fell to a disappointing 4–12 record.

The roster was overhauled again before the 2007 season—but this time, the changes worked. New starting quarterback Derek Anderson connected for more than 3,700 passing yards with 29 touchdowns. Veteran running back Jamal Lewis, who had signed with the Browns during the off-season, ran for 1,304 yards and 9 touchdowns. Young offensive tackle Joe Thomas was so effective on the line that he was in the running for Rookie of the Year honors. Suddenly, the Cleveland Browns had become one of the NFL's success stories of 2007.

But the team was most surprised when its much-

BRAYLON EDWARDS WAS DRAFTED BY CLEVELAND IN 2005 AND TRADED IN 2009

improved 10–6 record wasn't good enough to secure a spot in the playoffs. Cleveland needed the Indianapolis Colts to beat the Tennessee Titans in the final game of the season to ensure a Browns Wild Card berth, and many of the Browns' players huddled together to watch the game on television. No matter how loudly they cheered for the Colts, however, the Titans won. "Life can be cruel sometimes," kicker Phil Dawson said. "It sure does seem like everything has fallen into place for us this year. It's hard to imagine that it's over."

Cleveland fans began getting their hopes up for another shot at the playoffs in 2008, but those hopes were quickly dashed when the Browns lost their first three games. Anderson was so inconsistent under center that he was replaced in midseason by Brady Quinn. Although Lewis again ran for 1,000 yards and receiver Braylon Edwards made several big catches, it became evident that the Browns had more rebuilding to do.

It was also clear that they would have to rebuild without Crennel, who was fired after the Browns finished the season with a dismal 4–12 record. Eric Mangini was hired to take over for the 2009 season. Anderson and Lewis both suffered through subpar seasons as the team improved only enough to post a 5–11 record. But when Mangini's Browns ended the 2010 season with an embarrassing 41–9 loss at home to the Steelers and another 5–11 record, he, too, was let go. Mike Holmgren, a longtime NFL

Brownout

All of Cleveland cried on November 6, 1995. That was the day that Browns owner Art Modell told millions of loyal fans that he was moving their favorite team to Baltimore, Maryland, where state officials had promised they would build a brand-new stadium. Ironically, the very next day, the people of Cleveland voted to approve a tax that would have helped pay for renovations to Municipal Stadium. "I had no choice," the cash-strapped Modell said as he broke the news. The newspaper writers, television broadcasters, and mournful fans who camped out in front of the decaying Municipal Stadium made Modell out to be a villain who was looking to get rich quick. And indeed he did: Modell's new team, composed of all the Cleveland Browns players under contract when he left the city in 1995, became the Baltimore Ravens. In 2000, the Ravens won the Super Bowl, and three years later, Modell sold the franchise for $600 million. Cleveland's citizens eventually rebounded as well. In 1999, they welcomed a new Browns team to the $283-million Cleveland Browns Stadium.

THE BROWNS' RELOCATION WAS—AND REMAINS—A BITTER PILL FOR MANY FANS

KELLEN WINSLOW AND STEVE HEIDEN GAVE CLEVELAND A SOLID DUO AT TIGHT END

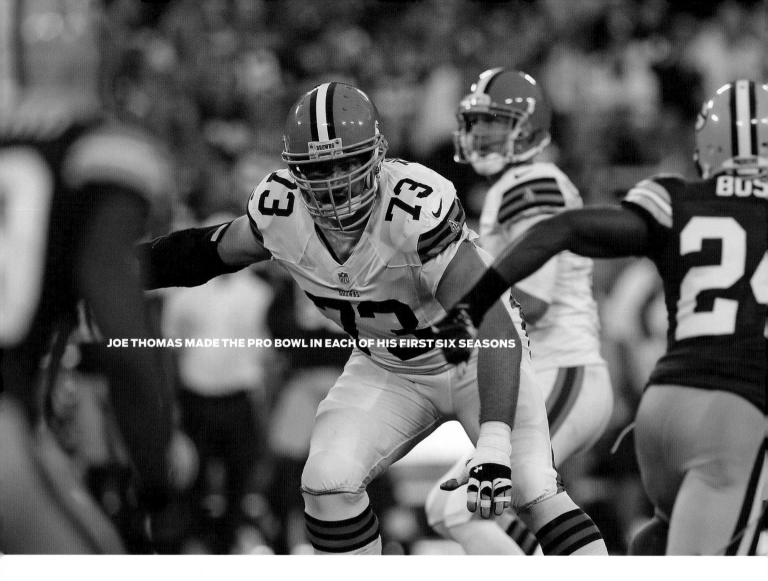

JOE THOMAS MADE THE PRO BOWL IN EACH OF HIS FIRST SIX SEASONS

coach who had become the Browns' president in 2009, was disappointed to have to make another coaching change so quickly—and was hopeful that he wouldn't have to do so again soon. "I don't want to do this again," he said. "Historically, if you look at teams that don't have to do this very much, they've been successful. It's very, very important that we get this right."

Although there were rumors that Holmgren himself would take over coaching duties, the Browns instead hired Pat Shurmur, who had spent the previous two seasons as the offensive coordinator of the St. Louis Rams. Shurmur took the reins of a young and inexperienced team eager to get back to the playoffs for the first time since 2002. But despite the best efforts of athletic quarterback Colt McCoy and scrappy running back Chris Ogbonnaya, the Browns faltered again and remained mired near the bottom of the standings in the AFC North, to which the Browns had been assigned during a 2002 restructuring.

But the Browns didn't plan to stay at the bottom of the heap much longer. With a crop of new

Bernie Kosar

QUARTERBACK / BROWNS SEASONS: 1985–93 / HEIGHT: 6-FOOT-5 / WEIGHT: 210 POUNDS

It wasn't always pretty when Bernie Kosar took the field as the Browns' quarterback. He launched the ball with an awkward, half-sidearm motion and was all but immobile in the pocket. But somehow he nearly always found his mark. Kosar, who grew up just south of Cleveland in Boardman, Ohio, signed with his hometown team after enjoying a celebrated college career at the University of Miami. He completed more than 300 passes in 1986, his first full season as a starter, and racked up almost 4,000 yards. During the 1990 and 1991 seasons, he set an NFL record by completing 308 consecutive passes without an interception. As Kosar developed into one of the best quarterbacks in the league, the Browns became a postseason powerhouse, marching into the AFC Championship Game three times in the late 1980s. His abilities on the field and his friendliness off it endeared Kosar to Browns fans. Cleveland Municipal Stadium often rocked to the sound of those fans singing their own version of the pop hit "Louie, Louie," with the catchy refrain changed to "Bernie, Bernie."

SHORT BUT POWERFUL, TRENT RICHARDSON HAD A STELLAR ROOKIE SEASON IN 2012

MOHAMED MASSAQUOI WAS KNOWN FOR HIS PHYSICAL STYLE OF PLAY

young players, including defensive tackle Phil Taylor and wide receiver Mohamed Massaquoi, emerging in Cleveland, the Browns and their fans began looking forward to ending their postseason drought. Unfortunately, their 4–12 record ended their 2011 season early again.

The Browns notched one more win in 2012, but even new ownership couldn't squeeze any more success out of the team. Former professional baseball pitcher Brandon Weeden was named Cleveland's starting quarterback in August 2012. His rough beginning evened out for 3,385 yards and 14 touchdowns, but he also threw 17 interceptions, something that concerned the management and led to rumors that Weeden's job would not be secure in 2013. "I expect competition," Weeden said. "That's the way professional sports are." Competing with franchise history was rookie running back Trent Richardson. In Week 2, he became the first in Browns history to rush for more than 100 yards and score both rushing and receiving touchdowns in a single game. Then, in Week 13, he brought his total number of touchdowns to nine, tying the rookie record of the legendary Jim Brown. Such heroic efforts were not enough to propel Cleveland past the mounting losses, and its playoff drought continued.

Whenever the Cleveland Browns make it back to the playoffs, their loyal fans will be ready to root for them, just as they have for more than 50 years. They celebrated with the Browns during the championship seasons of their glory days and urged them on as they struggled in recent years as well. Those fans will continue to cheer their Browns back to the Super Bowl, no matter how long it takes.

INDEX